Soulgasm
1.1

PURE PLEASURE
PURE PASSION
PURE LOVE
REVIVED

Soulgasm
1.1
**PURE PLEASURE
PURE PASSION
PURE LOVE
REVIVED**

TANYA DENISE

Love Wins Publishing
Chandler, Arizona
www.lovewinspub.com

Printed in the United States of America

First Printing, October 2022

To life...
To liberty...
To love....
Forever,
babygirl
xoxo

Soulgasm

—noun, verb \ˈsōl-ga-zəm\

A moment of pure, spiritual ecstasy.

When your body, soul, and entire being is in ecstasy.

An orgasm from the soul.

"How do you keep two souls apart when they felt so familiar from the very start?"

N.R. Hart

PROLOGUE

"F*** butterflies, I want flames!"

He pulled over. My breathing was labored. My heart beat fast. I was not afraid. I was eager. We were hungry!

He got out of the car and walked around to the passenger side. It was pitch black dark. No light anywhere, besides the beautiful stars in the sky and the radio station signature on the dashboard of the car where music softly played.

He opened my door, as always. I turned my body towards him to get out. He motioned for me to stay put. His sweat pants dropped to his ankles. He climbed into the car and on top of me.

I was ready for this. The moment I had laid back into his arms and his hand fell onto the top of my shirt and rested on my chest, I knew it was going down. We were on the mountain top, enjoying the nighttime city view, in a spot he had taken me to before. Things heated up pretty quickly in that spot this time. Touching, kissing, grabbing, squeezing, heavy breathing....we missed one another.

We made out in the car. That was my first time making out in a car. It was amazing!

He was not a stranger to me. Never had been. My mind could not put together what had happened between us in the past, what was happening in that moment, or what was about to happen.

I wanted him. No... I needed him! He needed me, too. I could tell that he needed me. Especially by the way his body melted into mine as he inserted himself.

My entire body trembled when he entered me. Welcome home, to the both of us. Passion filled the air and instantly I was taken into our zone.

We made love, again, for the first time, in a long time. Right there. Nothing and no one else mattered. It felt like it had been forever and it felt like it was just yesterday, simultaneously. Time suspended. We were in our zone, again, and it was everything.

He gave me all of him and I needed every bit. I gave him all of me, too. We held on tight as if our lives depended on one another in that moment.

He felt so damn good as he whispered into my ear. I sang a melody of lovemaking back to him. As I held onto him, I could feel the vibration of his manhood. The pressure was building.

His movement was sensual, rhythmic, focused, and calculated. He knew what he was doing. My body was in tune with his and we were making music. Our music. Our song. Our zone.

Our heartbeats were in sync, our breathing was labored. We both could feel it coming on. He thrust himself into me as if he was feeding me his soul! I wailed in pleasure. He growled as I pulled him into me.

Crescendo!!!

I had never made love in a car. Until that night.

"If anyone asked me "What is hell?" I would answer "Distance between people who love each other.'

Dear diary,

They say it is better to have loved and lost, than to have not loved at all. I am not so sure.

Things have come to an end in one case and I find myself thinking of another. I find myself reflecting, reminiscing, and thinking of the past, more specifically *him*.

I am not one to back track or circle back. When I am done, I am done. But...what if I wasn't done? What if we weren't done?

I find myself wondering what it was about him, about us, that was so different. Why haven't I been able to feel that with anyone else? Will I ever meet anyone who knows me like he did? Will I ever meet anyone who calmed the chaos in my world and made my heart skip a beat at the same time? Will I ever be touched the way he touched me? Will I ever be kissed the way he kissed me? Will I ever feel what I felt, again?

I feel like I am dying.... on the inside. I put on my brave face for the world. But inside something is missing.

I miss feeling invigorated and feeling alive. I miss being myself and being accepted in love. I miss feeling desired from the essence of my being. I miss being looked at, understood and heard...even when I utter no words. Will I ever have that again?

The Truth

Dear Love,

So many times I wanted to call you. I wanted to run to you. I wanted to seek shelter in my safe place - you. I would remember the comfort, the peace, the joy, the pleasure we shared. I knew a talk with you, a hug from you, a word from you would make it alright. It may have helped me leave sooner.

But then, I'd remember other things that made me feel insecure, unworthy, unsure, and unimportant - the reasons I ran from you. I also did not want to bring you any drama or jeopardize my safety. So, the only real safe place I had was prayer.

I wrapped myself in it and buckled down until the ride was over. When the ship wrecked, I was glad just to be alive. I had to gather the pieces of my heart, my dignity, and my faith so I could keep going.

I wanted to reach out days, weeks ago but I did not

know what to expect. I certainly did not expect to be where I am today.

Here I am not 48 hours from the last time. My body is sore. My heart is full. My mind is content. My soul is pleased.

Sexual healing is really a thing. You give me life and project healing from the inside out. Do you understand that something was missing in me and that is no longer is the case?

It's easy to give myself to you. It's like giving me to myself. It FEELS right. You already know but I need to express for my own sake how I have NEVER felt ANY of this with ANY one before you, or after.

I don't know what I am doing, so I need you to be careful because I can't afford another heartbreak. Be gentle (as you always have been) and rest assured I get it now. I get it.

I am in a vulnerable place. In my vulnerability, I gave myself to you again and that opened me up. There is no turning back at this point.

I needed everything you gave me and I have no regrets. I don't understand it. It contradicts my beliefs about so many things but it felt and feels right.

I have sacrificed and suffered long enough. I am tired in a way I cannot accurately describe. All I know is I gotta do what feels right for me.

Only you & God know your true intentions and I can only hope & pray that they are pure. I know what you said but it's never clear enough for me to take to heart. There is always an air of mystery. Either you'll make it plain over time, I will learn to navigate through the mysterious air, or something else will happen. In the meantime, I adore you. You hold a key that no one else holds. I hope you cherish it. The floodgates have reopened!

Forever,

Your babygirl

"It was like magic, the way you came into my life and made everything more beautiful."

More Truth

Dear Love,

You are a safe place for me. I realized today all my safe places eventually became unsafe. Not just the ones that I never should have let my guard down with but the ones who were supposed to be safe just cause (father, brothers, husband, etc.).

The deepest part of me is afraid of one day no longer having you, which also means I'd lose my safe place . I realized that today. I cried about it today. In the past, it was easier for me to walk away from you before you walked away from me.

I am vulnerable with you. I have opened myself and given you access that no one else has. Every time we lay together, we are trusting one another with our lives, literally. So, not only are you in my heart, and my mind, but my life in a huge way is in your hands. The cold part is, I can't do a damn thing about it. I could run...I tried that. Three times. Each time I ended up hurt and found myself right back in your arms.

Even after all the hell I've been through, I trust you in a way I don't trust anyone else. Be careful with that. As much healing as you have brought into my life, it could equally go the opposite direction on your part.

Laying on your chest, in your arms, and next to you feels like home. I really missed that. I have great peace and no pain. I feel safe, protected, understood, accepted, desired, and complete.

Thank you, for always taking your time with me....even when I blamed you for moving too slow. My brokenness looks like Kintsugi with you. You add that layer of gold to make my broken pieces look like a piece of art.

My pain dissipates with you. I need you in a way I've never needed anyone. In part, that scares me.

Your words replay in my mind and I can hear your

voice whispering in my ear. You said if I surrender, I'll never hurt again. Please don't lie to me.

I strive to believe in what I feel with you, especially when we are together. So many times, I've wondered if it's just part of the game. But if I've never felt what I feel with you, could you recreate that with someone else? How?

"What's meant for you will always feel natural, calm, and clear not forced, chaotic or confusing."

Hi!

It's me again.

I tried to journal or type in my "diary," this morning but I felt prompted to let this out here.

I just realized it has been a month since I have allowed myself to send love notes to you via email and to write poetry. Yes, "allowed." I have held back a bit trying to manage my emotions.

This morning, I looked around and I feel like my life is a mess. It is much more of a mess than it was when we met. When we met, I was about 5 months out of a relationship and was starting over. This time, I was about 5 weeks for certain out of another relationship - firm on the fact that I was done. Interesting, right?

Five is half of 10 and 10 is our number. Hmmmm.

All I know is you are an integral part of my healing. While everything around me seems loud and overwhelming, you are my peaceful place, my center, and my calm. It sounds good. It's poetic. It's romantic. It's deep. It's a lot of things but more than anything it's the truth.

I was on the verge of tears a moment ago as I looked around at everything I need to do and as I thought about everything I am behind on. I am not spiraling anymore but I still feel out of control and I do not like it. I could feel myself tearing at the seams and that is when I was led to write...or type...and not in my journal, but to you.

I can't break. I have no time to. The things that need to be done will get done and as you told me last week - one at a time. Sigh. Meanwhile, I have to focus on the bigger things that have been gifted to me.

What does this have to do with you? LOL I am just following the prompting I feel which it is helping me to recenter and refocus today.

I get emotional (and teary-eyed) when I reflect on the

many ways your presence has helped me heal, and evolve. You know me in ways no other human knows me and you know things that no one else knows. It used to scare me. Well, I am not afraid anymore.

I realize how much I need - yes, **need** (that was a hard one for me) you. When we first met and became involved, I used to pray that if things ended that they end sweetly. I never wanted to hurt you and I prayed that you wouldn't hurt me. If I hurt you when I ran from you, I apologize.

This time my prayer has nothing to do with an ending. You are forever part of me - embedded. I am marked and branded.

A girlfriend asked me if I thought you were "the one." Well, I don't believe in "the one." And that is what I told her. Not in the sense that she meant it.

However, you are and have been *the one* to touch me in places no one else has ever had access to. You have been *the one* to guide me out of my shell and into unfamiliar places that turned out to be alright, although I feared those places before you. You have been *the one* to see what others don't see or can't see. You have been *the one* to be close enough to provide the comfort I need but far enough to allow me to spread my wings and learn to fly.

You have been *the one* to speak to the essence of my being and activate parts of me that were untouched or parts that had been touched, broken, and destroyed. I was dying, on the inside, not once, but twice and you were *the one* sent to bring me back to life!

As I go through my process, I gotta trust the process. In my mind, I am eager to hurry up because I don't like the chaos around and I want to fix things, clear things up, get things on track the way I think they should be, etc. Sigh. But in the midst of it all, I am grateful that God allowed you to be here with me and as part of my life. Thank you for your patience, gentleness, and consistency in how you handle me. I value you. I appreciate you. I adore you. I am better now. TTYL

My love,

I've been touched before but not the way you touch me. I've missed others before but not the way I've missed you. I've kissed but ain't really kissed....or been kissed.

It's not only I don't like to do it. I've never really done it. You've tried and I've fought it because my mind was made that it's just something I don't like or do.

Last night, another wall came down. I felt fear and anxiety because old pain was exposed. It was pain I thought I had dealt with until I felt it again last night.

No one has ever taken the time to talk with me and walk with me through my own garden. They pass through for selfish gain, blind to the deeper hidden pain and other parts of me. I learned to accept it and move forward.

But you....you are something else. You are truly a Godsend. One of my angels on earth. You chose to stay, when you could have run, like the others. You even chose to receive me again, after I ran from you, ran from us. I am eternally grateful for you.

Remember, I hated sex. It was a chore. Kissing was no different. Guys who didn't know me tried to force their tongues down my throat and I hated it. Some grabbed me by the back of my head trying to hold me in place...forcing me!! Repulsive!

Everything was fast ....sex...touch...a kiss....relationship. There was no intimacy. There was no love making. The two men I married enjoyed f***ing me but never made love to me.

Yea, I got mine here and there but it was surface level. No depth. No substance. No connection. Nothing like you, nothing like us.

I lived with a man for almost four years and he still didn't know me like you do. He never wanted to

KNOW me. I did things with, for, and to him out of obligation.

The way you explained kissing was a little scary... only because it's unfamiliar. It's brand new. You took your time walking me through it like with everything else. Yea, I still feel fear from time to time, however I trust you. The fear feeling has become my natural response. It's a radar and a guard to warn me, to protect. I don't need it with you, yet I feel it at times. I literally have to remind every part of me that it's okay, it's you, not them.

I'm like putty in your hands. Even when I feel fear I KNOW when I just let go it's alright on the other side. Thank you, again, for your patience and gentleness.

I stepped into my womanhood on a deeper level when we met. The rose bud is blooming with, for, and because of you. Chains were broken. Walls are still coming down. I'm free. Free to spread my wings and fly....and soar. Like an eagle on a mission, after tiring

from soaring before. The freedom of the wind beneath my its wings, it returns to its nest - home.
I flew away fast ...in fear...but I came back....home.

*****

I laughed on at the start of this year as I threw all that damn lingerie in the trash. I didn't need it anymore. I no longer have to perform. It's no longer an act. I can play my part, naturally, authentically, with you. I can just BE and with you it's safe and okay. Home.

I needed you, again, and didn't realize it until it happened. I needed what you gave me from the inside out. You've taken my broken pieces and instead of throwing them at me or adding to them, you've helped me bring together what's needed and let go of the rest. Like Kintsugi....the Japanese art....my cracks are filled with gold because of and through you.

Last night, you healed a deep wound. My ex told me the trauma I faced as a child was my fault. I knew it wasn't but for him to say it cut deep. Last night, you told me it wasn't my fault right as the voices tried to invade our time by reminding me about it.

Just like satan takes everything that's good and from God and tries to pervert it or make it bad....you've taken what hurt me & made it feel good. You've flipped things in more ways than you know. Like gently redirecting a child walking the wrong way....you reach for my hand, literally, and guide me the right way.

I don't know how you do it. I am grateful and I appreciate you. I adore you.

Forever,
babygirl

"My soul has always had a space that I couldn't claim, I couldn't name; then you came along and I understood that it always belonged to you."

Dear diary,

He is amazing.

I thought I had been in love before but I have never known love like this. Not in human form. Not with a man.

Patient love. Gentle love. Kind love. Enduring love.

He has a way with me that shows me myself without making me feel bad about myself.

I have endured a lot and I have overcome a lot. The residue from my experience sometimes comes to the surface and it is not pretty. It is an indication that healing is still in order and I am open to that because I want to be the best version of myself.

I simply needed a safe place. A safe place to be, feel, share, and become. I have found it. In him and with him. As crazy as it may seem, this is what I need. I needed it then and I need it now. Nothing has ever felt more right at my core. I have to trust that. I have to trust God.

This man knows me and the only way he could know me the way he does is by divine access. Granted, he reads well and has more experience than I do, but there have been so many things that he should not know and he does.

He gives me that gentle nudge of reassurance when I need it, when it's necessary, not when I think I need it and I am fully aware that he doesn't have to. Sometimes, I think I would have given up on myself if I were him but he hasn't given up and although one time I remember him sounding tired as he talked me off the ledge, ultimately, he's so patient, calm, strategic, and careful how he deals with me and guides me.

He does not enable my unhealthy coping strategies. He shows up. He gives his time, which is more valuable than anything money could buy. But he does not feed the unhealthy parts of me at all. He doesn't intentionally trigger them either.

This journey is about me more than anything. I want to get what he came to teach me. Clearly, he came to teach me something.

I don't drive in reverse. I never go back to anyone...well not before him. He is special to me and what I feel with and for him I have never felt before. This might be the first time that I have experienced true love.

"If I were to live a thousand years,
I would belong to him in all of them."

Dear Love,

I woke up this morning with you. I don't even know what that means or how to explain it but I woke up this morning with you.

God reminded me about something. He showed me myself. This was pertaining to the relationship between Jesus and me, you, or anyone who believes, accepts, and confesses Jesus as Lord.

Ultimately, God showed me how He ever directly says, "I love you" in the Bible. We learn that He loves us, however through relationship with Him.

My relationship with you represents the closest thing to love I have known, in a relationship with a man. Men have told me they love me but their actions did not match their words. If that was love, I never want it again. Of course, I have learned it wasn't love at all.

Love is patient, love is kind. You are patient, you are

kind. Love does not envy, it does not boast, it is not proud. You do not envy, boast or walk in pride. Love does not dishonor others, it is not self-seeking, it is not easily angered, it keeps no record of wrongs. You do not dishonor me or others. You are not self-seeking, not easily angered and keep no record of my wrongs.

Love does not delight in evil but rejoices with the truth. Love always protects, always trusts, always hopes, always perseveres. Love never fails. You do not delight in evil but rejoice with the truth. You rejoice when I recognize truth. You always protect me; the way you handle me, even the way you touch or hold my face, or grab or touch my face.

You don't tell me what I want to hear, you tell me what I need to know. God does the same. He doesn't coddle us or give in to us. Not at all. You are the same way with me and it works.

You trust me, never questioning my choices or decisions or my whereabouts. You always hope I get it, see it, feel it - whatever IT is.

You persevere...with me ... when I have doubted, ran, thrown a fit, tried to hide, been afraid. You're right there, calm, cool, collected, and certain.

My relationship with you represents the closest thing to love I have known.

I am learning and unlearning. I am losing myself and finding myself. All of it intrigues me and scares me. I trust you and fear you at the same time. My relationship with you is a reflection of my relationship with God. Learning, unlearning, losing, finding, intrigued, scared, trusting, and afraid. Yep.

I am afraid to hold on and afraid to let go. I am afraid to be with you and afraid to be without you. Just like with God.

These things you already know. You could only know if God granted you access and you could only have access if there is purpose attached to it.

You have represented my healing & growth from the start. Like Jesus. You place no requirements or demands on me. You knock. You wait. Like Jesus.

You are gentle with me. Like Jesus. You don't expose my wounds or brokenness, yet as they are revealed you cover them with your presence...like Jesus.

My relationship with you represents the closest thing to love I have known. You are the closest thing I know to love.

My lover, my friend,

I am so grateful for you it makes me emotional. How could I not love you? You didn't have to stop here. You didn't have to stay here. You didn't have to deal with the mess or "dirty table" that those before you (and after unfortunately) created. You could have looked at me, saw the scars & wounds, got you some, and moved on.

You could have taken advantage of me being naïve & gullible. I could've just been a victim... of your love spell...A victim of the erotic passage of passion you bring. But you injected me with you & have stayed to help me manage my symptoms & side effects. You feed me in doses...carefully, strategically, lovingly.

How could I not love you? You taught me love. I used to think it was flowers, candy, date nights, getaways, family functions, roles and rules and sacrifice. But it's none of those.

When the door is wide open and my cat does not go beyond the threshold, it speaks to her commitment and her knowing where home is. A couple of times, she went out, not far, but it was cold and she even experienced a threat from a Tom cat so she ran back home, quickly. Now, I can leave the door wide open and she doesn't stray, although she has freedom to. This is home and she knows it. Sound familiar?

I didn't come here to love you but I do. I didn't even come to experience the level of healing and freedom I've had with you. I got so much more than I signed up for. And I love every bit, even the uncomfortable parts because once I conquer them, I'm gonna be that much better!

You are amazing. You are a gift to me. You are my guardian angel on earth. You set the bar and laid the foundation. The stuff that used to matter just doesn't anymore.

I appreciate you. There is nothing superficial about

it. I could just be next to you and that's enough. Of course, my insides crave more and it's because you're a part of me. When you're away too long, it feels like something is missing! I was literally dying....falling apart at the seams but reconciling with you got me all the way right!

I'm still shaking a lil bit but I'm taking steps. I'm moving in your direction and letting go in places I've held on in. You said you got me. I'm holding onto those words for dear life!

XOXO bg

"I belong to you. I've belonged to you since the beginning, since before I even knew I did."

Dear Love,

You unravel me.
Layer by layer.
Down to the bare bone.
I'm naked before you.
Exposed. Unashamed. Fragile.

You see inside of me and you see through me. You see my wounds, my weakness, my insecurity, my vulnerability, my flaws, and all.
And you're still here.

You beheld my essence. You saw beneath the noise & chaos. You connected with and to the purest parts of me.

You've never thrown anything in my face or intentionally made me feel any kind of way because of what happened to me or choices I've made. You've embraced me, all of me, and I'm eternally grateful.

I'm weak in your presence and I realize I just have to be. I can take off the mask with you. I can take off the cape with you. I can let my hair down and be free.

Trembling, I keep taking steps forward as I remind myself that it's safe here. You could have caused damage, taken advantage, and dropped me. Instead, you've taken my hand, you've sat beside me, and you've helped me unpack and sort through things. It's been uncomfortable, yet liberating. So liberating.

Freedom. I feel free with you! I get lost with and in you! Your energy fills me up, comforts and strengthens me.

You have taught me so much about me, about life, about love. I cannot imagine life without you so I won't. I need what we share and I savor every moment! I see you, taste you, smell you, feel you, and hear you, with my eyes closed. My soul is not just tied to yours; it is intertwined. I'm too entangled to ever be without you.

So, I'm letting go of trying to understand. I'm letting go of trying to make it make sense. God knows I'm more grateful for you than I can express. I cherish our time together. I appreciate you very much. I absolutely adore you! And I will continue to remind you and remind myself.

Thank you for your patience. Thank you for being so gentle, yet firm, and understanding. Thank you for not seeing the ugly parts of me and walking away. I hank you for kissing my wounds and loving me through my healing. Thank you for being careful with my heart.

bg

"When I am with you the only place
I'd rather be is closer."

Hello Love,

In response to lunch on Tuesday and our chat last night....

Yes, I was frustrated. I was also embarrassed. I felt uncomfortable that you know me better than I know myself.

Before accepting all of it, I needed to analyze the information. Not because I don't trust you but because I have never had a man tell me about me and be right. I needed to make sure you were right and I was not just accepting what you were telling me because of how I feel about you.

Not only have I never had a man tell me about me and be right, but I have also never had a man talk me through the things you talk me through. I have never met a man willing to stay around long enough to guide me through my own stuff, point things out, help me unwrap, uncover, and sort through things.

It's like the analogy you shared with me from Dondre Whitfield. A man sitting at a table that someone else ate from and seeing a mess before him and being expected to pay for the table for a meal he didn't get to enjoy. I am the table, the broken and messy table. When we met, I had a broken heart and buried trauma. When I ran and jumped into a toxic marriage, I re-injured myself and suffered more abuse and more trauma. I added to my own injuries. Then, I returned more broken and more of a mess. But I never expected you to pay the price for any of the damage. I am grateful you didn't get up and walk away from the table. Thank you for seeing beyond the mess.

I am happy, hurting, and healing at the same time. Everything in me wants to completely relax and trust this part of my journey with you, yet there is a part of me telling me to be careful.

You have not given me any reason to be afraid. You have not given me any reason to be concerned other than the fact that you do not communicate the way I prefer and think I need. You have never outright stated your intention. You have never directly said how you feel. That part keeps me guarded and that part influenced me to run from you the last time.

What keeps me here, intrigued, engaged, and involved now is how I feel when I am with you. I can have feelings for you and go about my business but how I feel with you does not compare to anything in this world.

I he way I felt when I heard your voice after so many years... The things you said that I wish you would have said back them...... The way it filled in holes I did not even know I had.

The way I felt when we embraced when we saw one another after so many years.... The way I felt when you took my hands into your hands... The way I felt when you were walking me back to my car and got close behind me. I felt your breath on my neck as you grabbed my waist to pull me back to you. The way you brought me back to life on the inside.... I can't make that up. I can't create that on my own or with anyone else.

The fact that I can't stay mad at you. The fact that your touch gives me peace. The fact that I miss you when you are away even when I don't express it. The fact that I sleep better with you next to me. The fact that my body starts to orgasm before you even enter me. The way my body responds to you. The way you know me.....

This stuff cannot be made up! It's not lust. It's not infatuation. It's not a phase. I thought it would wear off. I thought it was the age difference and you being more experienced. I even tried to meet, talk to and be with other men and it's just not the same.

I am breaking all the rules I know as far as seeing someone or dating or being intimate. You have a lot of access and a lot of pull. I have expressed more than I probably should have where my feelings are concerned and there is no more chase - my heart has been captured. I can't fake that. I can't play with that.

I don't know how. All I know is I love how I feel with you and I don't wanna be without this feeling. So, I pray and go about my day, savoring every moment shared and experienced with you.

I know that you are supposed to be here. I know that you are connected to my purpose and my healing and God knows I want to heal completely. I wanna move beyond that invisible blockage that often hinders me from moving forward. I wanna move beyond the fear and the residue from the past pain that I thought I was over.

You don't have to be here and you don't have to put up with my process, yet you are here and you put up with it. Why? Maybe I am just another assignment for you by God and if so, I know that if I have to ever carry on without you God will carry me, cover me, and see me through. In the meantime, you are a blessing to me and my life and I will not take advantage of that.

I have felt intimidated by you a few times and Tuesday was one of those moments. I know that was not your intention and I appreciate your continued patience as I work through my stuff. It's not a sob story; you know I've been severely disappointed so much that trusting with no qualms is one of the scariest feelings in the world. But I am pushing past it. I am doing it afraid because I want to be completely free.

Do I trust you? Most of the time. The crazy part is every time I lay with you, I am trusting you with my whole life, so if I can trust you with my entire life, why not everything else?!

XOXO bg

Dear love of my life,

It never fails.
You never fail...with me.

The last few weeks I fought it.
I suppressed feelings and desires.
I refrained from reaching out as much.
I refused to write emails to you.
I had to check myself to protect myself.

I joined the dating app 3/28.
My inbox was flooded.
I deleted the dating app 3/30.
48 hours of online madness.

Within that time frame, I gave my number to eight guys. I met two in person. Both misrepresented. Both didn't want to be my friend. Both wanted more and both made a move. Both were rejected without hesitation.

As of Monday (one week), two of the eight remain in contact. I predict they too will fall off. In fact, God already told me they are gonna fall off. Can you believe that? I heard it as clear as day.

It sure helped me keep my mind off you a bit. It also helped me keep handle on my desire for you. I didn't desire them sexually and I did not become intimate with any of them or even get close to it. That part of me is closed off to anyone else. Maybe others can share themselves with multiple people at a time but I can't. I've tried and it doesn't work for me.

I've had so many conversations in my head about you and about this and about us. I've tried to convince myself of things that all of me cannot settle on.

I really don't know what I'm doing, what we are doing. I do know that right now I can't stop it and deep down I don't want to.

The distractions help me keep my emotions in check. They keep me from feeling needy or wanting to be under you all the time.

I'm open about it because I'm open to you. No secrets. No hidden agendas. No ulterior motives. From day one.

It's never a ploy to make you jealous or anything. You're not even the jealous type and I love that about you. What's crazy is, you usually know when something is going on anyway. Both times I call myself going on a date with another man, you called me. You felt it. I love that and it reminds me why I just need to leave any other man alone.

Last night, I was in my zone until I fell asleep. I was surrounded by an invisible presence that I could feel so strongly that as we parted ways, I burst into tears. They flowed from my eyes until I reached the 60 freeway.

My skin was sensitive to my own touch and to the air. My legs were still shaking. My heartbeat labored and my heart swollen.

But this morning I can't feel it. Whatever that means.

Why are you here? How long do I have you? What will I do without you?

That just triggered more tears....Damn!

Have a good day.

bg

P.S. I LOVE YOU

Last night. Mmmmmm.

You pleasured me to no end! I still feel you. I'm still high!

If you had no intention at all on loving me the way I've grown to love you, then why would you open me up so wide?

If you had no intention on staying in my life, then why would you put your imprint on my heart & my womanhood.

Yea, there is an imprint. I'm marked... by you. It's like the lock to a residential unit. Only the owner has the key. Others have tried to gain access and stake a claim but my body literally rejected one and the rest of me rejected others.

Nobody knows my body like you, so why share it or

give it to anyone else?!

Nobody knows my heart like you, so why share it or give it to anyone else?!

In my mind, I have two versions of you. Version 1....all mine. What you give me, what we share, is ours and ours only. The faithful, highly emotional, in tune and connected man that you are can only bring the level of intensity and passion we share to me because it's focused....for me.

Version 2...just one of the few. What you give me, you give to many, and I'm only lucky in my term because I don't know better. The disconnected, distracted, wounded parts of you are careful with me, yet not focused or in a place to give me undivided attention.

Maybe it's you, maybe it's me, but to maintain balance you will deliver what you carry occasionally to the next woman, a more ready woman....and the next woman...

As I look at you trying to determine which version you

really are, my mind and heart can't understand how you could give anyone else what you give me. That fire, that passion, the essence of your manhood.... is MINE! It's ours and nobody else's!

But I wonder....Does your heart come with it? Am I just time and space that you share? Or have I earned a place IN your heart?

Tell me it's not just sex. Tell me it's not just a passionate love affair. Tell me it's impossible to feel this anywhere other than between me and you!

I mean, is it as good for you as it is for me? Do you feel the flame and the electrical charge of when we get close? Do you feel what I feel every time you touch me? Do you feel what I feel as we come together and the tip of your pressure meets the mouth of my womanhood?

You breathing on me literally makes me weak and sends vibrations all throughout my body! When our lips touch, when your tongue touches my lips, I fall apart from the inside. What is that?

It's not a game. It's not made up. It's not me being extra. It's what I feel and have felt since we connected and before we ever met face to face.

You entering me is like plugging me up to life source! It's like your manhood is a missing body part of mine because when you enter me it's the perfect fit. I feel you, I feel me, and it's blended.

Every part of my woman parts is pleasured when we join. When you release into me, I experience a different type of connection, an impartation to the conclusion of the soulgasm in progress! Your orgasm becomes my orgasm. Mmmmmm. It's so good, I shed tears!!

I have no control of you, or of me. You've set a high, invisible bar. It's so high, is it even possible for another man to reach it? You set it that high so you must be planning to maintain it. I need this. We need this. Let's never let it end. XOXO

My one true love,

I've been wined & dined, admired, and adored by other men who were completely infatuated with me but none of them compare to you. They gave me everything I thought I wanted but you give me what I need from the inside out. While I have desired more from you, I am grateful for every bit that I receive and sometimes I'm unsure if I can even handle you at full proof.

It's not that I can't be with anyone else. It's not that options are unavailable. It's not that there aren't men who are trying to win me over. Then and now.

It's just that my heart chose you, again.

Last time, I thought I was just caught up and I needed to jump off the ride you had me on. This time, I'm on the ride and enjoying it full throttle. I want everything that comes with it because you've shown me that it's safe here.

Yea, I still feel fear at times and my natural response to what I feel is run, hide, or pull back. Yet, I still come to you. Naked & afraid, I come. Uncertain, I come. Walking in my healing, I come. Peacefully and thankfully, I come.

Running can be fatal. Hiding is honestly impossible. Pulling back offers a temporary layer of protection for my heart.

You are my comfort. You are my peace. You are my safe place. You are my escape. You are my pleasure. You are my lover. You are my friend. You are my teacher. My heart is in your hands.

Do you understand how I lose control when we are close? Do you understand how I leave this earth when you touch me, when you enter me, and we become one? It's a new dimension. It's another world. I've only gone with you and I only wanna go with you because I know I'm safe. I've learned what's on the other side when we enter our zone.

I wish I knew what it was like to love you unafraid. I wish I knew what it was like to love you having never experienced a broken heart. I wish I knew exactly how you feel about me. I wish you'd love me like you've never loved anyone else.

I love hearing from you, looking at you, being with you. I love how you touch and hold my hand. I love how you touch my face. I love how you caress my body. Lord, have mercy! My God, how I adore you....and I'm sick with it!

XOXO

"You can wash my scent from your skin but it will never leave your soul."

Hello my love,

I try to compartmentalize this. It helps me focus and function better. I don't want to think more into it than what it is. I've had that mind frame from day one. But when I do that, you come around and say something that shakes up my box. Then, I'm back to feelings and fighting to focus.

Round one, I told myself it was just sex. Great sex. Amazing, mind-blowing sex, but that's it. I was not and could not be the leading lady in your life. I accepted it and rolled with it as long as I could. Yes, I cared. Yes, I loved you. I just had to put it in perspective based on you never asking or telling me you wanted more with me.

This round....I needed you. More than I realized until I felt your arms around me and later felt you inside of me. I did not care if there was anyone else in your life. No disrespect but that is where I was. I needed you and nothing and no one else mattered.

My head is still in that space. The main reason is because of where I am in my process. And as long as I "don't care" I also can't be hurt the way I know it could hurt.

The challenge is the inconsistency. You'll pull me in then pull back. I try to just be grateful that I hear from you every day. And it has been every day since we reconnected. I appreciate that. You know that.

I also make sure to not sweat the small stuff or trip because there is nothing for me to really trip about. I've got things I desire and some days I wish this & that but I've got enough on my plate to tend to so I hone in on that. This is why last night I said the inconsistency could drive me crazy IF I let it.

I think where I'm most messed up at is not knowing. Not knowing how you feel. Not knowing your thoughts or intent. Not knowing how any of this is supposed to go.

I feel vulnerable and weak expressing the fact that I really don't know how it's supposed to go but it's true and you know it's true.

Ultimately, I appreciate you for being a safe place for me to be vulnerable, weak, transparent, emotional, etc. I thank God it's you and no one else because I'm a predator's dream. Like a young gazelle....grazing, basking in the sun, clueless to everything around, yet runs.....RUNS.....anytime she feels or senses a threat. But if he's nice enough, kind enough, and moves slowly to get close, she is tricked...killed, and captured.

I have been captured and damn near killed one too many times. I hope you understand why the urge to run is still present.

"I fit in his arms like he was born to hold me."

Sir,

So, I guess you were calling earlier because you knew I wouldn't hear from you the rest of the night?

Just when I think I got this and I can do it, I realize I don't got this and I can't do it. I front...a lot and often, with and for you.

I'm too emotionally invested. I'm too vulnerable. It has become what it was before.

I've given you too much access, control, and power. I've fooled myself, again. I've accepted crumbs of all sizes and pressed them together to make a cake...one that doesn't exist. It's not a cake....it is crumbs mushed together to look like a cake. I'm fooling myself!

My soul has been crying all night. She woke me up with her cries. I've felt this before and I can't afford it this time.

How can you hear her crying and let her? You said you got me....but that is not how it feels.

On Friday, as I was driving, I thought back to Wednesday when I told you I needed to know how you felt and you said what you felt had nothing to do with me and I didn't need to know. You reminded me that you won't feel like I do. You took me around a mountain instead of just telling me what's what. As usual and again.

I've been here with you before. I don't like how it feels.

It isn't right for you to not be clear with me. It isn't right for you to deliberately choose not to be upfront. You are very strategic about what you say and don't say. That's intentional.

At first, I thought on Wednesday how perhaps I didn't wanna know how you really feel about me because if it's not remotely what I think then it's gonna hurt. And who wants to feel pain on purpose?!

But if it's more than what my mind sometimes concludes I need to know that before I demand my heart to chill the hell out and let this go!!

Then, I thought today (excuse me for being raw and blunt but), f*** that! I wanna know! I deserve to know! I wanna know how you feel, what you feel, and what the hell is going on. At least then I can decide what to do with the truth. But....you won't even give me that.

You give me crumbs....like I'm desperate and starving. You give a little here and there. You pull me in and push me back, again and again, and I let you.

I let you because I love you.

I didn't mean to love you though. Not then and not now. I didn't mean to show up after almost six years apart and rekindle a flame that clearly never went out. My soul led me back to you after my heart ripped the mask off. Underneath the mask was a heart that yearned to feel you again. It didn't care about anything or anyone else...it was so strong that it violated everything I thought I knew and believed. It went against who I said I was.... to be where it wanted to be.

But it's not right for you to KNOW how I feel and for you to not be clear with me!! It's not right for you to make love to me, and to have my heart in the palm of your hand and not let me know whether you intend to be here or not in the way that I need.

It's not right.

You give me a lot, when you give to me. But you give me the most IN that moment...and only in that moment. The other times you give me mind f***s. Because I'm often dickmatized or dickzzy aka dick dizzy as if I done fell and hit my damn head! So, you talk around points that I need. You know the power you possess and how it paralyzes me to the point I can't even think straight.

Here's the thing....if you told me that you don't love me and you just enjoy what we do, it would make some sort of sense and I could better equip myself and navigate things on my end. I could keep my emotions in check as I accept this being just that. But every time I tell myself that and try to back up, you call me out or draw me closer as if you don't want me to pull away. When the distance is to protect my own heart and keep my head clear to avoid things like this.....unable to sleep, tossing and turning, thinking way too much about you, trying to get this female crying on the inside to shut the hell up!

If you told me that you like me more than you planned, yet you know I'm not *her*, I'm not the woman that calms your soul the way you calm mine, yet you still care, and wanna keep doing what we do - that would explain a lot and make it easier for me. It would also help me to be careful to not close myself or heart off.

Because right now it's closed. There is a whole security system on my heart. My heart and my body are not available to anyone....naturally reserved for you. Even not knowing how you feel.

But I did that before. A whole two years of being loyal, faithful, committed, to man who was not committed to me.

And listen – I'm not saying I want a commitment at this time. In fact, I don't even feel like I know enough about you to request, expect, or desire a damn commitment. Honestly. We haven't spent enough time really really talking. It's usually you talking. When I say something, you turn it into a lesson or lecture.

As much as you know, sometimes I feel like you don't know me at all. And there's a blockage where I can't know you on the level you know me. You don't let me in. You haven't granted me access. You give what you want when you want. You won't even be frank and tell me how you feel, what's going on, or what your intent is even if it's nothing!! It's not right and it's starting to hurt more than I anticipated. Something has to give.

It's been 19 days. This is the longest since we've reconnected. I feel like I'm dying inside and I hate feeling like this.

I had a hotel room for three nights and you couldn't sacrifice one night....I would have done it for you with no hesitation. But as you've made clear, you don't feel what I feel.

But what is it that you feel? Why are you here?

"They slipped briskly into an intimacy from which they never recovered."

Hey,

Here we go, again.....

I can't help but express myself with you.
You fill me up and top me off.
I smile from the inside out.
There's no feeling like what I feel with you.
I get upset and throw fits, then you so carefully and gently reel me back in. I hate it and love it.
In your presence I have great peace.
I needed you badly last night! Thank you for coming.
I'm so fulfilled. My mind is at ease.
My heart is full. I'm still floating.
I want this feeling forever!

I am eternally grateful for you. I hope I give you at least half of what you give me.

I still feel you. I still smell you. I still taste you. I wish you could roll over on top of me right now and give me more!

I love when you look at me and talk to me when you're in me deeply. My body craves you!

I love when you touch that place inside of me that no one else has touched. You take me on a journey to ecstasy.

No one has ever made me feel the way you do. No one ever will.

This is forever...

Forever babygirl

Dear diary,

It never fails. I get all bent out of shape and in my feelings, doubting and thinking the worse. Then, he calls or he just shows up and whatever anger or frustration I felt it goes away. I get stupid. I lose my thoughts. Literally.

He doesn't even have to say anything. When the phone rings, I am checked. If he shows up, when I see him, I melt on the inside. I simply can't stay mad at him and sometimes that makes me mad.

I am still afraid of him and he asked me why. Am I so f***ed up from my past that I can't fully embrace this experience? I try and I try so hard. I don't even know what normal and healthy love looks like. What I thought was normal and healthy wasn't that at all so when I think something ain't right is it really right?

Sigh.

I have to resort to how I feel and trust it. And this is not a shallow feeling. What I feel with and for this man is so deep. The way he centers me. The way he calms me. The way he makes all of the chaos around. His presence brings me so much peace. His touch and I am not talking sexually. He can touch my hand or my face and it is magical.

I am scared. I am scared to mess up again. I am scared to be hurt again. I am scared to miss a sign or symptom. I am scared to disappoint God. I am scared to lose what I have with this man because it is one of the greatest feelings I have experienced.

My love,

If you're not my forever, I don't know what I'll do because I can't imagine my life without you.

Tomorrow is not promised, so while we have today, I want to remind you that I appreciate you and I adore you.

It's the 1st of a new month, my birthday month, and as I've prayed and reflected on months passed, I can't help but be grateful. You came into my life at a time when I needed you most, then and now. Some days I wonder how I made it this long and how did I go so far without you.

At the same time, everything unfolded on purpose with purpose. The things I went through before you and within the last several years have only caused me to appreciate you more.

Thank you for not giving up on me. Thank you for

forgiving me. Thank you for being available and coming back into my life. Thank you for believing in me. Thank you for never judging me. Thank you for sharing you with me.

Thank you for not throwing me aside and disregarding me. Thank you for being patient with me. You know the ugly things about me and yet you're still here. You've seen every part of me, from every angle, and you're still here.

I don't know how long I'll have you, but I will cherish every moment. Just sharing time and space with you is a blessing I don't take for granted. To be your lover is a greater honor! You give me the deepest part of you and your essence gives me life! To give you me is the greatest gift because no one else has that access. It's my pleasure to be your pleasure and receive pleasure from you.

I've tried to fill in the time with the distraction and part time company of others here and there but nothing compares to you. I'm over it. I'm not even interested in wasting my breath to answer another man's call. Another man's voice is my ear is like clawing a chalkboard. Your voice is my ear is a melody.

My heart says you. Only you. So only you it is.

As I enter a new year, I'm eager to see what tomorrow holds. And today I'm so happy you're in my life. I hope and pray I give you at least half of what you give me in peace, pleasure, comfort, and joy!

I don't know what it is or what it will be but I know I love how I feel with you. Thank you for all that you are and all that you aren't. Thank you for handling me with care. Thank you for guiding me, teaching me, coaching me, covering me, loving me, and letting me be me!

Love is freedom and you let me fly....but I always fly back to you. Your hands are the nest for my heart. It can safely rest there.

Even when I prayed, I believe I heard God say my

heart is safe here. That gave me the assurance I needed.

bg

HIM

Them: How do you feel about him?

Me: I love him.

Them: How do you know?

Me: How do I not know.

I feel him in my soul.

He was familiar from the first time we connected. In fact, we were already connected before that.

When we met, it was as if we were meeting again. I felt peace with him. A great peace.

The first time I saw his face, he wasn't a stranger. I knew him and just didn't know how.

The first time he wrapped his arms around me, time stood still. Not only did I feel peace but I felt safe.

He knew things about me I never told him. He told me my dreams as if he was a part of them ...because he was.

In one dream that I had many years ago, I could never see the man's face. He described this dream to me one day....out of nowhere. As he did so, tears fell from my eyes because he was describing what I had never told him. As he walked me through MY dream, suddenly I saw the face. It was him.

When he touched me for the first time, my heartbeat changed and every time he touches me it does the same. It doesn't skip a beat. It doesn't become labored. It slows down. It becomes calm. I become calm. My thoughts, my emotions, all of me. It's like I'm not even breathing, yet clearly, I am.

It's hard to think in his presence. It's as if I don't need to think in those moments because he does it for me. He speaks how I feel. He knows me in ways no man has and he knew without me telling him.

He's a reader. I'm an open book...in a language most can't translate. Other men are illiterate. To me, he's a genius.

He patiently sits next to me as I unpack my stuff.... stuff I've carried for years. Stuff I've needed to let go of and leave behind. He's erased my heartache and replaced it with heartfelt moments.

It's like a movie... in real life. It's my life and sometimes I can't believe it. Sometimes I want to go all in and be completely consumed by him. Sometimes I wonder if I can handle that.

What's crazy is this hasn't been like anything else. He doesn't wine & dine me. He doesn't lavish me with flowers or gifts. Yes, we've gone on dates, out to eat, been in public places during the day and at night. It's not a secret love affair. We've spent nights together, been to each other's jobs, etc. However, we haven't shared other common things typical relationships share.

I've been married and I lived with those men and they never knew me like he does. I never felt with them or any man what I feel with him.

When we come together, it's magical. I leave here. I enter our zone. It's filled with passion and pleasure. I never part from his presence empty. He fills me up and satisfies my soul. He gives me life!! He gives me something to hold onto and I hold on!

My body knows him. He knows my body. My spirit knows him. He knows my spirit. My heart knows him. He knows my heart.

He's led me to soulgasms - they're deeper than orgasms - without touching me. Yep, it's deep. It's amazing. I giggle at the thought.

The anticipation of him entering me....words can't describe. And when he enters, we blend. I can't tell where I end and where he begins because it's like we're truly one. The sensation of pleasure isn't just inside, it's all over. My skin becomes sensitive. In that moment you can touch my nose or toe and I'll orgasm.

He activates something in me and I love it. No man before him had that ability and I don't think another man ever will.

I adore him.

We don't look like what we share. Whatever that means. You just wouldn't know that we do what we do when you see us. We both have a bit of a nerdy flair. But there is another side...and for me, only he sees that side of me.

There is an age difference between us. He is older and it doesn't matter. He is my friend. He is my lover. He is my comforter. He is my teacher. He is my counselor. He is my heart.

When I am away from him, I feel sick sometimes. I have to intentionally keep busy or sit still and have a flashback to activate the comfort he is and not focus on how empty I think I am when he is not around.

There's just nothing like being in his presence. Nowhere else gives me that peace.

I don't like being away from. I don't like too much time to pass without hearing from him or seeing him. I hate that I ever walked away from him.

I know he cares for me so I imagine now that my walking away hurt him. I never meant to hurt him. I never want to hurt him or see him hurt. I thought he didn't care and that I didn't matter much. I thought I had gassed him up and tricked myself into believing it was more than what it was.

Coming back to him proved otherwise. It proved we weren't done. We had unfinished business. It proved I never stopped loving him.

When I saw him again after all of those years, that spark became a flame. It was him. It's always been him and it always will be.

To: You
From: Me
Time: 7:30 am
Mood: Relaxed and grateful
Dedication: "Best of Me" by Anthony Hamilton

Dear diary, lol

It's amazing how I feel when we part ways. I am always full....giddy, and grateful. I usually blush on my drive home as I listen to our playlist and talk to God about you.

I replay our time together as I take deep, slow breaths, taking it all in.

I noticed last night, however, how I switch between Latanya and Tanya.

Tanya still gets nervous around you. Latanya is all in. I notice my own internal shift. Like a switch...from nervous and awkward to relaxed and free.

While you were pumping gas, and my door was closed I had to tell Tanya to relax and I asked, "What are you nervous about?"

Latanya has to remind her to calm down and go deeper....to get out of my head and get in the moment.

Touching you helps. When I put my hand on your back or your leg, the shift happens. Or when you touch me.

Anyway, it's always a pleasure and a joy to be with you. You invited me to dinner but I wasn't hungry (for food) and I wasn't planning to eat food. I was just grateful (and excited) for the time with you.

One thing I appreciate with us is the level of comfort. I don't have to dress a certain way. I don't have to fix up. I don't have to perform or put on. I can throw anything on and we're still gonna have our time with no fuss. I can be me and you can be you....silly, funny, intelligent, analytical, emotional, gentle, chill, and loving you!

I'm STILL smiling inside & out. High on you.

Thank you for being my safe place. Thank you for being you.

"He is my favorite sensation."

Hello handsome,

I love when you're on top of me and you tell me to look at you. I love when you stare deeply into my soul as you give me you. I love being skin to skin, eye to eye, soul to soul...with you.

The thing is - I didn't always love it. It used to scare me. I used to think you were putting a spell on me. Sometimes I wanted you to just be quiet and keep giving it to me. Now, she's like, "Look into me.... Talk to me DADDY."

Because your words resonate with the essence of my being. You speak to the deepest parts of me. You make my body do things it never did before you. It yearns for you. It knows you and you know it.

Touching you is like touching me....I need your touch. I need you... and I've never needed anyone, like this.

I know I've said it before; however, I have to express it

again - I love when you release life into me. My soulgasms are AMAZING, however feeling *your* release and knowing pleasure has consumed you, invigorates me.

I LOVE when you come inside of me....always have, always will. To some it may seem disgusting. And for me to share that with any other man it was disgusting but not with you. It's been that way from jump.

In that moment, we are both so open and vulnerable. We are trusting one another with our lives! My life is your hands then and there and your life is in my hands then and there. That is powerful.

I can feel your release physically and I feel it in my soul, as well. I love it so much that you can release without me getting mine first and I'm ok with it because I get mine when you get yours! I can't help it. It turns me on to the max.

When I say I love it, I LOVE IT! It's a feeling I've never shared with anyone! The mere thought arouses me when we are apart. Like right now.....Mmmmmm.

Stay right there...each time...for a moment longer. Let me take it all in as you get it all out. Mmmmmm.

You release life into me, literally. And I give birth to new feelings and new things. Hell, 20 years ago, maybe even 10 years ago, Id wanna have your baby because it's that damn good! And when it's that good it can make you do crazy things...

My crazy thing is choosing to give you me, and choosing you and only you. I know I have freedom, however with my freedom you are my heart's song. I fly, I soar, and I always return...to you. It's been you.

I'm in love with your soul. How I feel is deep within. It is beyond my head and my heart. You're in my spirit, a part of me that longs to reconcile with you often. Yea, you're still with me when we part ways...yet there is nothing like when we come together....when we cum together.

I'm in love with the part of you I can't see. The part I FEEL when you look into my eyes, when you breathe on my neck, when you touch my hand, or my face, when you grab me in the middle of the night and pull me close to you.

How I feel is from the inside, out. If I could unzip you, open you up, and see those parts, see your soul, it'd probably blind me. The light, the energy, the power would be so strong!

As much as I chose you, you chose me, too. The question is how did you know it was me?! How did you know we'd enter other dimensions together? How did you know you'd pour into me and I'd express it so vividly & freely back to you and to the world? How did you know there'd be passion & fire between us? How did you know I'd come back and be unable to ever truly let go?

You are part of me and I am part of you, forever. You are etched in my soul, grafted in my heart, forever. This is a love affair of a lifetime. It's music. It's poetry.

It's like a movie. It's spiritual. It's natural. It's healing. It's adventure. It's spontaneous. It's fun. It's unadulterated. It's uninhibited. It's passionate. It's erotic. It's us. It's Soulgasm.

"Have enough courage to trust love one more time and always one more time."

BOUND BY LOVE

My heart,

I went to bed mad at myself. I woke up sad. Last night hurt. Deeply.

I'm trying hard to focus on what is and not what isn't.

Here is how I feel:

I'm on standby.
I'm the last-minute choice.
We can never plan anything...lunch, dinner, an outing, or time together. You never just say yes to me. It's always "we will see" or "I will let you know" and many times I end up knowing by a no show, a no call or me following up.

You know how important it is for me to hear from you, especially after we've come together, yet some days you go all day with little to no communication.

You've got a whole life that I know little about. Your job and your family are clearly important to you. You're often busy or have things to do.

I'm a speck in your universe.

I get what's available or what's left. You don't carve out time for me, even when I give you advance notice or invitation. If nothing else is going on, then I might get lucky and get some time.

Me....I'll stop just about anything to be with you. I'll cancel appointments and rearrange my day. I'll pull over to respond to your text so too much time doesn't pass between your message and my response.

I think about you often. Sometimes all day. I make it a point to let you know so you don't have to wonder.

When good news happens, you're the 1st person I wanna share it with. When bad news happens, you're the 1st person I wanna run to.

You're more than a speck in my universe. From one angle, you are my universe. Herein lies the problem.

Here I am, again....in this space of realizing I've stepped out into the deep. I didn't guard my heart like God said. And today my heart hurts.

I'm resilient. My bounce back game is strong. Sometimes that's a problem, too.

I bounce back. I forgive. I let it go. I get over it or moved passed it.

It happens again. The hurt. So, I repeat my process. Forgive, let go, get over it, move passed it, again.

In my mind, I wanna make demands but love won't let me. In my hurt, I wanna be mad but love won't let me. In defense, I wanna go off and be entertained by someone else, but love won't let me.

Love is freedom but it's holding me hostage.

Sometimes I wish I meant to you what you mean to me. That's never how this goes. And the ones who feel as deeply in return get rejected. Why is it this way?

Why is it that men have felt for me what I feel for you but I don't feel for them how I feel for you? Is love ever matched?

I still don't understand why you're here. It's not just for me. You're getting something out of this, too. Just please don't keep me on reserve until you decide you're done with me, leaving me with pieces of a broken heart. Because as bad as I wanna run....right now....love won't let me.

EMOTIONAL UNLOAD

Hi,

It's me. It's us.

This morning you sounded tired. Thank you for calling.

I really appreciate the time you take with me. I do not take that lightly. I see it and it means a lot to me.

Your efforts, your response, your showing up, your being present, your expressions, your attention, and your time are ALL recognized and appreciated.

I was a mess in my last letter. I apologize if it's ever draining or frustrating for you when you have these talks with me. I don't want to push you away with my mess. I am fighting to get passed this wall that I keep running into. This blockage that you didn't cause or create, yet you continue to help me break through.

I've prayed for whatever I need to get beyond this place and to get to the place where my mind and heart are in sync and Latanya & Tanya are in agreement without reservation. It's my goal and I am a goal slayer!

Thank you for being so patient.

When you called and I did not answer, I was in the restroom blowing my nose and wiping my face after a crying spell. Tanya told Latanya and God that she did not know if she was emotionally strong enough to stay on this journey with you. She's so guarded and so afraid, that even when it feels right and feels good, she questions it all. She just wants to protect us.

But I (Latanya) told her what I know and heard in prayer: You're not here to hurt us.

This new round with you is making clear the depth of the trauma I have experienced in relationships with men and its impact on my life. I had a broken heart when we met and you helped me heal. I hated sex and intimacy when we met and you changed that. I opened up in ways that were unfamiliar and it scared me. Because I didn't understand it, nor did I understand how I felt with and for you, I bolted and put myself in a position for more trauma to take place.

This time it tried to take me out literally! But I got out alive, I'm still here and I am so glad you're here with me, now.

I refuse to make you pay for what you did not do. I refuse to let fear run me or control me. I refuse to miss out on the experience with you because of what has happened to me.

You just recently told me to stop holding a grudge against myself. I am doing everything that I can to work through the stuff and to let what I need to let be, just be. If you haven't noticed, it is easier said than done, but I am doing - I am trying.

This morning you acknowledged how being emotional is part of me, it's who I am, and how there is nothing wrong with it. Tears raced down my cheeks when you said that. I have spent years fighting the emotions and keeping them bottled up. I was taunted in other relationships about being emotional. I thought there was something wrong with being emotional. I thought my emotions overwhelmed you. So, hearing you acknowledge and validate who I am was huge.

I came across memories where you told me you were teaching me to emote. How timely. Even then you were teaching me that it's okay to be emotional.

In the memories, I told you how I was afraid of how I felt and you said, "Don't be afraid of what you feel, be afraid of what you don't feel."

I feel so much with, for, and about you.

In fact, I have expressed this before but it is fitting for the moment.

I was starting to not feel. I felt myself becoming cold. I was dying inside...slowly and painfully. No one knew.

Seeing you again stirred something within, then coming together again gave me life! It awakened me - it was like mouth-to-mouth resuscitation! I felt alive again, instantly. Remember, I told you - I didn't feel guilt like I thought I would. I didn't feel like I had done anything wrong. I needed it. I needed you. I needed to feel, again.

Have I told you lately that I love you? Have I told you lately how amazing you are and how much you mean to me?

Well, I love you, you are amazing, and you mean more than I can express. As I read some of my past love letters to you, some of our old text messages, and recalled conversations, I realize how precious this experience with you has been. The emotions are just as intense, if not stronger. Nothing has faded or declined.

Hear me....last night, when I felt the urge to run - wanting to avoid the hurt I felt - I opened the Facebook dating app and stared at it. After a few minutes of Latanya versus Tanya, I closed it (without creating an account) because I don't want to talk to another man. I don't want to be with or around another man. I don't want to entertain or be entertained by another man. Period.

I don't want to fool myself again. We see how that turned out. And even when I dipped my toe in the water this year, there were sharks everywhere. I'm cool. Matter of fact, I am satisfied. While what we share unfolds and does its thing, there is plenty for me to focus on that doesn't have to involve another person or me using them to not be so caught up in my feelings about you.

So, I sat with my feelings last night for the first time in a real way. Instead of burying them and covering them with the shadow of another person, I sat with them. But as I sat with them, I got mad at myself. I tried to pray and fell asleep and woke up sad. Still sitting with my feelings.

On the bright side, I can feel. And 99.9999% of what

I feel, feels good. If I can just figure out how to marry my mind and heart so Latanya and Tanya are walking together in agreement, I will be GOOD!

I am trying my love. I am trying. Your kindness and patience are everything and mean so much! Thank you for not giving up on me or fussing at me when I have those moments.

By the way, before it has any room to grow into anything, I need to inform you that I love our talks and I love that you share things with me. I tell you everything - you're my male bestie. So, when you share, I am like a biscuit and you're gravy - I sop up everything you drop. HOWEVER -

You taught me that men and women can't be friends. The man had her or is waiting to have her. Right? So, please know that I am not particularly fond of you sharing when you talk with this or that "friend" of yours. You've shared bits and pieces of conversations you've had with "friends" and when you do that my mind begins to wonder - who is she? Did he have her or is he waiting to have her and where does that place me?

I am at a place with you where I am not seeing anyone else. I tried to make "friends" but based on what you taught me and what happened when I briefly tried, I am cool. A man is not trying to be my friend and I am not open, interested, or trying to sleep with anyone else. Plus, my heart is under lock & key.

That being said any indication of you doing whatever is a trigger and it hurts. Opposite sex "friends" don't exist, according to you. So, sometimes the way you word when you were "talking to a friend" gives me a vibe I am uncomfortable with.

Last round, we actually talked about and agreed to exclusivity. Of course, that is the preference for many reasons. But you've also taught me to not want anything from anyone they don't want to give. So, I don't want it if you don't want to give it. Because then you're giving it because I want it, not because you want it.

I trust that you are fully aware of my heart and my fidelity to you, to the point of being careful, cautious, guarded, and responsible with both.

On that note....I will close.

"Passion makes the world go round.
Love just makes it a safer place."

Baby, baby, baby, baby!

DADDY, DADDY, DADDY, DADDY!

My God in heaven...thank you!! For this man, for this experience, for this journey! Thank you for your grace & mercy!

To the love of my life, my one true lover....You gone have to do some real f'd up stuff to get me to leave you alone.

Listen here...

You give me that fire, baby!! I get lost with you and I love it!

That's my act right, my feel good, my do right, my all night, my fix. I am addicted to you and like a feen I need it. The more I get, the more I want. It never gets old. Each high is brand new and sends me to a new place!!

On the bed, in the car, at the park, leg up, leg down, from the back, you on top, eyes open, eyes closed....daytime, nighttime, sunlight, moonlight...this right here.....is everything!

You can get it when you want it because I need it anyway, all day, every day! No lies.

Our scent....Mmmmm....

A heavenly mixture of sweetness...berries, candy, butterflies, rainbows, and suga.... dripping with pleasure.

You give me the most, and I love it so much!

I love you. I love you staring deeply into my soul, penetrating my core and feeding me you. You take nothing and give me everything. You fill me up again and again!

How did you know to love me like this? What we do together should be a crime and I love serving time....with you! What did I do to be served like this. Can't nobody do it like you!!

We don't even have to kiss. Foreplay is like every day because when I see you, I'm ready! Right then and there! I stay ready for you! And it never fails....you please me every time!!

Each time I feel brand new. You're taking me higher and higher....I wanna go...with you! Give me more...

You shoulda seen the way I sashayed through the store with residue of our juices between my legs. My hips swayed a bit more, my derriere felt firmer, I felt a lil taller, and my smile was fixated. I laughed and giggled along the way.

I am still floating....high off your lovin and I'm lovin every bit of it!

Forever,

Fa eva, eva

babygirl

"Love isn't something you find.
Love is something that finds you."

MATTER SO MUCH

My handsome lover,

One-hundred men could tell me I'm beautiful and it only matters when you tell me. My phone could blow up with likes, notifications, and messages from other men, but it only matters when it's you.

Why do you matter so much?

You stayed when others left. When others find out about my imperfections, they back away. When you found out, you stayed. Not only did you stay but you held me, you comforted me, you laughed with me, you talked to me, you gave me scripture, you gave me guidance, you held my hand.

You saw my baggage and still saw me. You told me you were trying to get to know me before the trauma, before the scars. Isn't that all anyone wants? To be seen, to be known, to be heard...before the hurt and pain.

I don't understand why you stayed but I am so grateful that you did. How could I not love you? How could I not appreciate you? I came back to me with you. I can be me with you. All of me....naked and unashamed. Literally.

We get skin to skin, heart to heart, eye to eye...souls intertwined. No layers in between. All of you. All of me. Raw.

You take your time with me. Every time. And if there is not enough time, you won't even begin. You even stop if you need to, to make sure I'm all there with you. Every time.

You're gentle with me. Even when the beast in you awakens...and he triggers the beast in me, you put him in check. He wants to devour me....in a good way, but still. You touch me gently, you kiss me gently, you stroke me gently. He watches.

You taught me love on a new level. A deeper level and

a higher level at the same time. I had to unlearn and learn many things. I had to push passed blockages and hindrances. When I became stuck or afraid, you nudged me to keep going....to the other side. And every time I get stuck or afraid, you're there to encourage me to take the next step.

You've been an integral part of my healing and growth journey. You guided me to the place of facing & embracing my healing. You've helped me heal ... from wounds you didn't cause.

You guided me into sexual healing. What was a stain, a scar, and a bad taste in my mouth, has become brand new. What I once hated, I now love, because of you.

You taught me how to feel. You taught me not to suppress how I feel but to manage it. You taught me how to let go. You taught me how to be free. You taught me how to slow down...in everything.

You taught me how to trust you. You taught me what

love is and what it ain't. You taught me connection, chemistry, passion, & ecstasy. You taught me spontaneity, adventure, & pleasure. You taught me what it feels like to make love.

How could I not love you?

Forever,
babygirl

Heyyyyy love,

You were in my dreams last night and when I awakened with a smile you were right next me. How lucky am I to dream about you and to wake up from the dream already in your arms?

I love sleeping next to you. I feel safe and shielded. I feel calm and peace. My heart is full and all is well. Even with the light off.

Did you know that ever since I was attacked by him while I was asleep, I sleep with the light on? The first time I turned it off and slept all night in peace was after us. After being with you again. I did well that night but on the 2nd night I turned the light back on. I've tried to sleep with it off here and there but occasionally I've still had nightmares & flashbacks of the attack.

Last night the lights were off and you were here. No nightmares and I even had a sweet dream about you....while literally sleeping in your arms.

Thank you for picking me up from the airport and for staying with me. I needed it and you must have known. I had told myself I'd go with your flow...if it was a straight pick up and drop off then you knew that's what I needed. I wasn't gonna ask for more or less. I was just gonna trust your judgment and be grateful.

You knew that I needed more and you gave me that. For me, it was the perfect ending to an emotionally taxing weekend. You are my safe place, my comforter, my peace and then some and I needed all of that last night. Thank you.

I felt proud and a hint of shame watching you fix and clean the vacuum and vents. Proud because I love seeing a man be a man. Your hands got dirty and I cringed, I also smiled because it was nothing to you. I felt shame because there is so much that I need to do around the house....and got the nerve to travel so much. Some days I don't know what to do first because there's so much to do.

If I can share...just as I was learning to accept help and operate in partnership and not carry the weight on my own, my life shifted. I went from someone else being the primary breadwinner back to having to figure it all out on my own, again. I went from someone else picking up the slack and helping wherever needed to trying to keep up with it all, again. This time it's been different and I admit sometimes I struggle.

I cried the first time I had to put gas in my car again because I was used to someone else doing it. I liked someone else doing it. I had finally let go just to have to pick things up and hold on again. The transition this time is a trip. That is all I'm saying.

I just thank you for getting things straight for me last night. It may not have been much to you but you didn't have to do what you did. I appreciate it. More than you know.

Ohhhhhh to be in my spot....after the gates of hell tried me this weekend....to be in the comfort and safety of your arms was just what I needed. To feel your heartbeat as my own heartbeat came into sync. To fall asleep in your arms. To hold you. To feel you. To pray over you. It was EVERYTHING!

We fell asleep right away, too. I think it was a matter of seconds before I heard you snoring, then I fell into deep sleep, too.

It had only been 11 days...felt like forever though. Then again it felt like yesterday, too. Does that make sense? You're in me and on me no matter what I do or where I go. I think of you in all I do. I'm just so grateful that I get to be part of your life and you get to be part of mine.

You touch me where hands cannot reach and you kiss me where lips cannot go. Because of you I shine a bit brighter from the inside out! XOXO

Dear Love,

I have never met a man like you. I am intrigued by you, inspired by you, taken by you. I am curious about you, invigorated by you, blessed to just know you.

When we are apart, it is often difficult for me, yet I manage. I hold onto the last time, as I await the next time that I get to see you, smell you, touch you.

There is no greater feeling than how I feel when I am with you. I don't understand it. Sometimes I don't like it. But it is what it is.

You are embedded in me. Your fingerprint is etched in my soul. No one can look at me the way you do. No one can see me the way you do. No one can have me the way you do.

No one else could have caused me to violate my beliefs and go against what I knew. But anything to reconnect with you. Anything.

You shook up my beliefs and challenged me to question what I thought I knew, to explore things on another level spiritually. It's uncomfortable at times but I get it.

I pray for you. With no guilt, no shame, no condemnation. Everything about being with you feels right. I cherish it and hold it near and dear.

No heat. No smoke. No pressure. No fuss. No rush. No hurry. No worry.

All faith, all hope, all trust, all thankfulness, all peace, and all love - pure, honest, peaceful love.

~babygirl

Dear Love,

Welcome to new. New month. New day. New opportunity. New mindset.

This morning I was reflecting and I thanked God for second chances. His mercy and grace create opportunities that we sometimes overlook. I don't want to be His ungrateful child and I don't want to be an ungrateful person. So, with each new day I choose to be grateful.

Today I am grateful for a second chance with you. What do I mean? Many days and nights I recalled the stained memory in my heart and soul. The way I felt with you. The time we shared. How much you meant to me. I was convinced that it was a once-in-a-lifetime thing. I did not think I'd ever see you, hear your voice, or be with you again.

I couldn't wrap my finger around WHY we happened or what it all meant. I was just grateful for the experience and deep within longed for something similar, again.

I searched for it and ultimately searched for you I guess in others. Nothing there. Usually, when I am done, I don't look back or go back. I have never broken up with anyone and gotten back together. I had never dated anyone and called things off and went back to try again. Not before you.

I guess my soul knew what I needed and that is what led me to reach out that sweet day. Oh, sweet December.

I took a chance. You could have been married. You could have been seeing someone else seriously. I did not care. I took a chance and I am glad that I did.

I remain grateful for a second chance. A second chance to feel again. To see again. To heal again. To breathe again. To come alive again. And it happened with you, through you, because of you, again. XOXO

Dear Love,

You are not everything I was looking for. I had no clear idea what I was looking for and I didn't see you coming.

You get under my skin...you rub me the right way and the wrong way at the same time. You steady me and make me unsteady.

You're unpredictable and predictable. You make believe in love and question everything I thought I knew about love.

You make me feel reckless and out of control, wild and free. I'm inexplicably drawn to you. You're the reason I can rest and the reason I can't sleep at night.

XOXO
bg

"We loved with a love that was more than love."

My love,

Last night was wonderful. I really enjoyed the hilltop city view while nestled under your arm. I enjoyed our conversation and laughter. I loved walking through the park, holding hands, taking pictures to capture the beauty of the evening. Every moment we share is sweet to me and only gets sweeter.

My heart is full. My mind is clear. I'm almost speechless and that's a first.

You have taught me to slow down. When I'm with you, everything in me becomes calm. The urgency of anything else going on doesn't matter when we are together. You are literally my escape.

Even when we make love....I like how you center me and bring my focus back to taking it all in and slowing down. Being present in the moment.

When we kiss, you lovingly stop me when I'm eager to

move fast....then, you slowly come in flooding my entire being with passion and peace.

Thank you for the way you handle me. Thank you for the way you know me. Thank you for the way you love on me. XOXO

Hello love,

Here I am...
In the middle of the ocean...floating.....reflecting...and thinking of you.

Today I realize I have released three books this month (only 18 days in) and all three are bestsellers. Even in the excitement of my success, I'm laying here.... thinking about you.

Last night, as I slept to the gentle roll of the ocean under the ship, I wished you were next to me. Some days, I don't know which part of this is most exciting....being with you or looking forward to being with you, again. I'm gonna go with the first option. Being with you is definitely the cake. But looking forward to being with you is the smell of the cake in the oven, almost done, while hungry!

I can smell it, I can feel the warmth, and I can damn near taste it melting in my mouth already.

I have learned to stop trying to figure things out between us though. I've decided I'm just gonna live and the energy will flow and fit where it's supposed to.

Getting anxious does me no good. Getting upset does me no good. Waiting around does me no good.

This is gonna sound crazy but I have to express it for emphasis....

If I never saw you again or never talked with you again, my heart would break in a million pieces. However, I'd be eternally grateful to have experienced you not once, but twice. I never imagined a second round, a second chance. But here it is. So, I'd allow the memory of the energy and passion we've shared the first round and now the second round, to mend my heart. The memories would carry me through but they could never replace having you. XOXO

OUR ZONE

My love,

I love when we go to our zone. I love when you take me to our zone. I love how you love me down and fill me up in our zone.

Do I need to tell you how you put it on me like it was brand new, like I was brand new? Like it was the first time. Like it was the last time. Last night and especially this morning. I was crying, praying, and all.

I love how you take your time with me. I love how you speak softly to me and guide me through from beginning to end.

I feel amazing. I needed every bit of what you gave and didn't even know that I needed it. Sound familiar?

My body hurts and I feel like going to the gym is gonna break me all the way down today because I already had a full body workout. Damn!

141

I especially love and appreciate moments we share like laying side by side on the pillow and talking. I loved when you laid your head on my pillow and I laid my face on your head. Your head was near my bosom and my hand was on your neck and I prayed for you as you fell asleep.

This may all seem redundant but it's all very true and I never want to take any of it for granted. In case you ever wonder, in case you have a doubt, it's here in writing. And it's all true. Everything I feel. Everything we do. The world will know how my heart beats for you! How you call my soul to the surface. How you speak to the essence of my being. How my body responds to you. How when we come together, we blend and merge into one. I feel you but I feel me when I feel you.

The exchange of passion and emotion. The synchronicity of pleasure. We make love! And today we made love so profoundly.

You are forever etched in my soul, embedded in my heart, and flowing through my veins. You've gone beneath the shell and touched my beginning and my end. You have filled me up with so much of you there is no room for another man. Not now. Not ever.

You are a part of me and I am a part of you. Apart from one another we're just existing. Together we come alive, in a new way!

I love you. I love us. I love this.

If you were trying to remind me of anything in the last 24 hours, well I hadn't forgotten but notice was given and I got served!

It's you and only you. It's yours and only yours.

Forever....your babygirl

"All that we love deeply becomes a part of us."

Hello there handsome,

No man had ever made love to me....before you. It was never about me with them. I was just a body. From the first sexual encounter of my life, I was used for their pleasure.

From our first intimate encounter and still, you pleasure me. I remember you telling me that you didn't need my help and to just lay back. Even two days ago you told me to just receive.

I smile from the inside out with you. This ain't even about sex, it's deeper. In fact, on many occasions you've stopped mid-session to remind me that you don't want my sex, causing me to shift gears. You refuse to f*** me or just have sex with me and I love that about you.

You've had to teach me how to make love. And you've taught me not only to receive but to feel and to be present in the moment. You've taught me that I don't need to perform with you. It's not an act, anyway, it's an experience.

Even during our adventurous encounters, you make love to me...everywhere and anywhere we go, WE make love and you make sure we do....every time.

At one point in my life, I couldn't tell the difference between being f***ed, having sex, and making love. Now, it's clear. And as I said in the beginning, no man has ever made love to me....before you.

Everything you told me in the beginning that you believed about sex and lovemaking has proven true. You're quite skilled at what you do. You are lovemaking.

I'm in tears as I reflect....you're so gentle with me, so focused, so intentional. My pleasure is your pleasure. The way you touch my hand. The way you touch my cheek. Damn! I know I have said it a thousand times and perhaps this is how it's supposed to be but understand it has never been this way for me, before you!

You speak to me with such loving care. You have never raised your voice at me. You've never called me out of my name. You've never commanded or demanded anything of me or from me. You've never been a threat in any way.

I feel safe with you. Safe in your arms. Safe in your presence. Safe letting you in.

You pull things out of me that were hidden. Even things I didn't know was there. You challenge me in thought and you help me dissect my emotions to understand them better. No one knows me like you. No one holds me like you. No one deserves me like you.

You've put in the time and the work....to read, to study, to know me. Does anyone experience this more than once in a lifetime? Does anyone find a soulgasm connection more than once? Can the passion and pleasure we share be recreated at the same magnitude? I'm not convinced. I don't think I will ever find this anywhere with anyone. I'm sold.

Dear diary,

I'm a sucker for him. When he calls or texts me, I wish there was a hidden camera so he could see just how I silly and excited I get. Oh, and when it's time to see him, I play it cool but my insides are jumping and flipping with joy!

It's been this way from the start. Eight years later and he still has this effect on me.

Today I told God for the first time that I think I want a chance to know my lover on another level and I asked God to make the purpose of what we share very clear then show us how to navigate it. I've never asked this before. I've never prayed about us being together before. I just don't wanna waste his time or mine if we are occupying space in one another's hearts that was intended for someone else. I also don't want to mess things up between us because I like what we share when it's us.

I love him and there is no sense in trying to keep that in. I want him around. He's the main man in my life, already, and I wanna know what it's like to be the main woman in his life on a serious tip.

He's been single for so long that I'm not sure he wants more with any woman. Maybe he likes his life just the way it is. But I know I want more for myself in the long run and putting him into that picture seems fitting.

No other man knows me like him. No other man comforts me like him. No other man inspires me like him. And no other man pleases me like him. If I could have life AND love with him, I think it would be great. But I only want it if I'm supposed to have it and ain't no need to rush. He taught me that....he taught me to go slow. In everything. Go slow when kissing, go slow when making love, go slow when dating. Go slow.

He has taught me a lot. Too much for me to account for in this moment. But he can tell me anything and I will believe him. I don't think he'd lie to me. He's too calculated. He's very intentional about what he says or doesn't say. There is a method to his madness for sure. He's never led me wrong or misguided me. When I listen to him, it works, no matter what it is.

I do not understand him but I want to. He's often unpredictable, mysterious, consistent at being inconsistent. I never know which way he's coming or what he's going to do. But in the end, I get to see him and be with him so I fall back and let him do what he does.

I don't have the energy to figure out what he's not ready to reveal or disclose, how he feels, what he wants, etc. I just pray, hold my peace, and be his peace. I will never demand anything of him. I don't think I could anyway. I don't have to be that way with him and if I was that way, he probably wouldn't put up with it.

I just want to enjoy him. I'm so thankful for him. Sometimes I'm concerned because he doesn't share or express a lot but I feel him at times and don't know how to interpret what I feel so I just pray. He'll tell me he's great and wonderful although I feel otherwise... I just pray. Quietly.

I feel it when we are apart and I feel it when I lay hands on him when he's next to me. The other day I felt how tired he was. Not physically but in the inside. As he laid on my pillow, I laid my head on his, kissed him, and put my hand on his neck and prayed. I don't know if my prayers help him at all but I'm not gonna stop praying for him.

He's often occupied with so much. Work. His family. Those two alone consume him. And he never complains. I wish he'd let me in closer and more often. In the meantime, I'm just grateful to have him in my life and vow to not be the one to bring the heat or the smoke.

This is precious to me. He is precious to me. I will protect what's precious the best way I know how.

Forever,

babygirl

My dear, sweet lover,

While in the midst of making love last night, you whispered and encouraged me to give you my "pain." You said I still carry a wound and I need to release it to you so I could receive all that's on the other side...you said to give it to you....just like I gave you me and my heart.

I'm not exactly sure how to do what you've asked or if I did it or not last night. In that moment though tears welled up in my eyes and I felt a deeper connection to you. I literally had a vision of my chest opening up and our bodies merging.

Then, you said, "All...."

You told me to give it all to you....not him.

An electric surge flooded my body and I entered an orgasmic song that lingered from your very slow, concentrated, calculated, intentional motions. Tears slowly and gently crawled down my cheeks.

There I was crying....during love making, again, with you.

I've cried before with another but it was because I hated what was happening. I didn't wanna be there. I was filled with regret, disgust and more. He didn't even know that I was crying. He was too consumed with himself.

But that wasn't the case with you. The first time I cried or this time. In fact, I couldn't control the tears. I couldn't stop them. And you felt me crying. You hadn't even looked at me, yet told me to hold onto to you tighter and whispered "I gotchu."

Then, the whimper....the proof of the tears started because how did you know....how do you ever know?

How have you taken what hurt me and used it to heal me? How have you helped mend the broken parts of me?

Give you my pain? What do you do with it? And how? If I'm holding 10 pounds of pain and I give it to you what happens? How do you take what has hurt me and turn it around?

How do you do what only Jesus is supposed to do?

How is any of this possible when we are by standard fornicating? How are we in sin, yet coming together feels so right? So necessary.

Even our scent is sweet. The aroma from the mix of our love juice is like expensive perfume. And I never feel empty after we come together. I always feel full....complete. I never feel guilty or convicted either. I feel good every time. Like we are doing what we are supposed to do. Like we were made for each other.

I smile as I flashback to yesterday and how after what seemed like hours and hours of lovemaking, we climaxed together. Your release triggered my release and it was beautiful.

In fact, I could feel the build up to your release. It was so strong this time. And that excites me. I could feel your manhood get firmer and flex. Your breathing changed. Your motion was steady and fixated. I knew it was coming.

We were drenched in sweat. The bed was wet. Our bodies were entangled. Wrapped in passion, love, and ecstasy. It was incredible. It was invigorating. It was spiritual. It was us. It was soulgasmic.

I had an assignment related to our relationship. The task was to describe the relationship. Here it goes:

DESCRIBE THE RELATIONSHIP...

It's the sweetest, most intimate, and most freeing relationship I've ever had. He does whatever the hell he wants to do and so do I. No pressure. No stress No restrictions. No requirements. No demanding expectations. I only expect him to be him and he expects me to be me.

I tell him more than he tells me but it's by choice. It comes with being who I am and I don't know any other way to be. I feel safe with him so I naturally desire to share things with him....personal things, silly things, everything.

Would I like him to be more interested and excited and engaging? Sometimes. But more than anything I want him to be himself. Genuinely. I wanna get to know **him**. I don't want anymore actors or pretenders.

I don't want anyone playing any role. I don't want a cheerleader or a free rider. I want an advocate. I want an honest, lifelong friend. I want to know him differently and if who he is and who I am end up no longer blending the way we do, so be it. But as long as it does blend well, I'll accept it.

It's been a heck of a ride with this man and I have no regrets. I chose this. I chose him. I chose....not because I felt forced or obligated. Not to avoid being taken advantage of. I chose him from the beginning...and I continue to choose right now.

I was drawn to him. Literally. I thought it was for one thing and it ended up being so much more! He was never a stranger. The inner me was never afraid of him. I felt like I knew him all along.

Everything about us is very different than anything I've ever experienced. Sometimes it's difficult for me but I've learned to self soothe and to trust the journey.

I don't want anyone near me, with me, or in my life because they feel obligated or because I asked for it. I want them here because they want to be.

When he reaches out, when he texts me, when he calls, when he comes, it is because he wants to. Not because he's obligated. The best feeling is when you're with someone who wants to be with you. They choose to share their time, space, and energy. No one made them. Not a relationship or marriage vow. Not a baby. Just their heart and mind.

I don't want him (or any man) to commit to me because it's what I want. That's a potential recipe for disappointment. I've lived that. If he wants me to be the leading lady or the main chick or the only chick then I'm with it. That's how I'm wired. I'm not easy to spread. I'm too layered to separate parts of myself and share with multiple men. But I will never again ask a man to commit to me. He'll have to do it because he chooses to.

I've learned that at the end of the day if a man wants

to be faithful then he will be. If he wants to cheat, then he will. Whether there's a ring involved or not. No matter what a woman asks or expects or demands, he's gonna do what he wants. The key is we get to decide if we accept it or not.

Right now, I accept my own freedom. I accept my own healing. I invite to myself what I need even greater than what I think I want.

I accept that he has a life. I'm not his life. I'm thankful to be a part of it however. I have a life too and he gets to be a part of my life. All by choice. My choice.

If he wants me to know something, he'll tell me. I keep my questions to a minimum and I'm ok with it. That's probably a trauma response. I don't like being lied to. So, if I don't ask, I don't give him or anyone an opportunity to lie to me. I'm safe there ...in my own bubble. That works for me right now.

I feel safe in accepting that if he chooses to be with someone else, then he did what he wants to do. There is nothing I do can stop that. The same goes for me. He has never told me not to be with anyone else. I choose not to because of who I am and because my heart is invested here, with him.

We should all be able to do what we want to do without guilt, shame, pressure, fear, judgment and so on. Freedom. Even God doesn't make us do anything. We choose. If God doesn't make us, why should we try to make others do anything?

I've learned that in relationships we don't own the other person. We just get to share a portion of life with them. You can be committed without pressure. You can choose what is safe for you and your heart and the person you care about.

In my case, he knows how I feel. My God, he led me here. He knows that I care deeply about him. He knows that I adore him. He knows my ultimate desire and preference is to be exclusive. Now, he gets to choose if that works for him and if it's in alignment with how he feels and what he wants.

I trust God and his heart enough to believe he will not do anything to damage my heart. It's endured enough and he knows. He's the one who has helped my heart heal. Why would he so carefully help mend a heart then break it?

I've never felt more free interacting with a man. I've never felt safe on all levels with any other man.

Love isn't restrictive. Love is liberating. This connection, this feeling of freedom, this experience, this relationship, this journey, THIS is love.

Forever...and ever,
Always babygirl

"Our love story was written so many centuries ago
and to think after all that has happened,
we're just about to get to the good part."

I Corinthians 11:11